Pyramids of Egypt

Pyramids
of Egypt

Don Nardo

Watts LIBRARY

Franklin Watts
A Division of Scholastic Inc.
New York • Toronto • London • Auckland • Sydney
Mexico City • New Delhi • Hong Kong
Danbury, Connecticut

Note to readers: Definitions for words in **bold** can be found in the Glossary at the back of this book.

Photographs ©: Bridgeman Art Library International Ltd., London/New York: 31 (British Museum, London, UK/Ancient Art and Architecture Collection Ltd.), 41 (Egyptian National Museum, Cairo, Egypt); Corbis-Bettmann: 33 (Yann Arthus-Bertrand), 42 (Gianni Dagli Orti), 13 (Gian Berto Vanni), 47; Envision: 26 (Michael Howell); H. Armstrong Roberts, Inc.: 25; Mary Evans Picture Library: 38 (Edwin Wallace), 10, 34, 37, 48; National Geographic Image Collection: 24, 49 (Kenneth Garrett), 30 (C.F. Payne); Omni-Photo Communications: 15 (Tony Perrottet); Photodisc, Inc.: 16, 23, 44; Stock Montage, Inc.: 40; Stone: cover, 46 (Sylvain Grandadam), 2 (Will & Deni McIntyre), 5 top, 18 (Stephen Studd); Superstock, Inc.: 6, 9, 14; The Art Archive: 5 bottom, 21 (Dagli Orti), 20 (Dagli Orti/Archaeological Museum Naples); Wolfgang Käehler: 50.

The photograph on the cover shows the pyramid of Khafre. The photograph opposite the title page shows the pyramid of Menkaure.

Library of Congress Cataloging-in-Publication Data

Nardo, Don, 1947–
    Pyramids of Egypt / by Don Nardo
        p. cm. — (Watts library)
    Includes bibliographical references and index.
    ISBN 0-531-20359-X (lib. bdg.)   0-531-16226-5 (pbk.)
    1. Pyramids—Egypt. [1. Pyramids—Egypt. 2. Egypt—Antiquities.] I. Title. II. Series.
DT63 .N37 2001
932—dc21
                                                                                2001017967

Contents

The pyramids of Giza were built as the final resting places for three kings—Khufu, Khafre, and Menkaure.

Chapter One

Land of Pharaohs

In the hot desert sands of Giza, near Cairo, a group of immense stone pyramids towers into the sky. Because the surrounding area is mostly flat, the two largest pyramids can be seen for miles in all directions. At a distance, they look like tiny pointed mounds projecting above the horizon. But, moving closer and closer to them, the pyramids become more and more imposing and impressive, until finally they blot out most of the view of the deep-blue Egyptian sky.

Another Wonder of the World

Besides the Egyptian pyramids, which were built as tombs, the seven wonders of the ancient world included another magnificent burial monument. It was built about 350 B.C. for a Persian ruler named Mausolus by his wife. His name is the source of the term **mausoleum**, meaning "a large stone tomb."

Egypt's great stone pyramids are among the most famous and beautiful sights in the world. Every year many thousands of people from every corner of the globe visit Giza and gaze in awe at these majestic monuments, as people have for hundreds of generations. Indeed, the great pyramids are extremely old. In 130 B.C., a little over two thousand years ago, a Greek poet named Antipater of Sidon listed them as one of the "Seven Wonders of the World." Yet when he was a tourist visiting the pyramids, they were already immensely old. As incredible as it sounds, more centuries separated Antipater from the origins of these structures than separate us from Antipater. This is because Egypt is one of the oldest lands on Earth.

A Country of Extremes

In addition to being an old country, Egypt is a land marked by great extremes. Located in the northeastern corner of the continent of Africa, more than 90 percent of Egypt was—and still is—made up of **arid** desert wastelands. Winding like some monstrous snake through these dry areas, however, is the mighty Nile River. Its cool waters irrigate the narrow but highly fertile strip of land along its banks. Looking down from

an airplane, that rich strip of land resembles a huge green ribbon twisting through the parched desert sands.

In the beautiful and rich Nile Valley, the ancient Egyptians built a splendid civilization. Among their achievements was a system of writing, which they carved onto stone walls and other monuments and also set down on **papyrus**, a kind of paper made from a water plant. They also erected huge stone statues of gods and human rulers and built great palaces for these rulers to live in. Most impressive of all were the great pyramids, which over the years have come to be seen as the

In this photograph, the contrasting landscapes of Egypt—the arid desert and lush greenery—can be seen.

9

The Nile River

At a total length of 4,132 miles (6,650 kilometers), the Nile is the longest river in the world. The River has two sources—the Blue Nile and the White Nile. The Blue Nile begins in the highlands of Ethiopia while the White Nile comes from farther inland. The two rivers join together near Khartoum. The Nile flows to its mouth at the Mediterranean Sea, on Egypt's northern coast.

Menes is considered to be the first king of Egypt.

trademark—the major identifying feature—of ancient Egypt.

Egypt's rulers built more than ninety pyramids in all, most of them relatively small, but a few quite large. The majority of these were completed during the era that modern historians refer to as the Old Kingdom. It lasted from about 2700 to 2180 B.C., a period of roughly five centuries. Even then, Egypt was already very old. The region had originally been divided into two separate kingdoms, one in the south, the other in the north. Sometime between 3150 and 3100 B.C., Menes, a powerful king of the south, united the two kingdoms into one country. He established the first of its many dynasties. (A **dynasty** is a line of rulers belonging to a single family.) Eventually, Egyptian kings came to be called

pharaohs. Over time, more than two hundred pharaohs, representing over thirty dynasties, reigned in Egypt.

The Importance of a Proper Burial

Whether they were small or large, Egypt's pyramids all served the same purpose—they were tombs, usually for kings. Building pyramid-tombs became a custom among the pharaohs of the Old Kingdom. Some of the rulers of the Middle Kingdom, lasting from about 2050 to 1650 B.C., also made such tombs. This custom grew out of the increasingly elaborate burial rituals practiced by Egyptian royalty. Over time, their tombs became larger, or more highly decorated, or filled with more valuables—or all of these things.

In Egypt's earliest years, people thought that only a pharaoh, who was considered a living god, could attain **immortality**, or eternal life. Later, the Egyptians came to believe that all persons, whether rich or poor, had a chance of reaching the afterlife. There, they would enjoy eternal bliss in the heavenly realm governed by the god Osiris.

However, the privilege of entering the afterlife was not seen as automatic. The journey from the land of the living to that of the dead could only be assured by observing certain proper, time-honored rituals. The rituals included preserving the body and supplying offerings of food, utensils, clothes, and other materials to sustain the soul. The Egyptians also made sure that the body and material offerings were in a proper grave.

Early Royal Tombs

For rich people, especially the wealthiest of all—the pharaohs—a proper grave meant a large and lavishly supplied tomb. Before pyramids developed, such upper-class tombs took the form of a *mastaba*, a word meaning "bench." And indeed, these flat-topped rectangular structures resembled the simple benches many Egyptians keep outside their front doors. The mastabas of the early pharaohs were constructed of bricks composed of mud that had dried and hardened in the sun. Each mastaba had several chambers. For instance, the tomb of Aha, the second pharaoh of the First Dynasty, featured five rooms. The king's body, which was protected by a wooden coffin, lay in the middle room.

Unfortunately, building structures from mud bricks had one serious drawback. The weather rapidly made the brick mastabas crack and crumble. Because so many of these mastabas simply fell apart over time, those who could afford to do so eventually turned to using stone, which was much more permanent.

This practice of building mastabas from stone led to the appearance of the first pyramid-tomb. In the early years of the Old Kingdom, work began on an all-stone mastaba for the pharaoh Djoser (also called Zoser) at Sakkara, near Memphis. This structure underwent several changes and enlargements before it was finished. As a result, the final version consisted of six mastabas stacked on top of one another in layers, each higher layer smaller than the one below it, forming the world's

This mastaba is located near the pyramid of Khufu.

13

Built for King Djoser, the Step Pyramid became the first pyramid.

first pyramid. This structure fittingly has become known as the Step Pyramid.

The Great Age of Pyramid-Building

In the generations following Djoser, many of his successors attempted to match or surpass his impressive achievement. Their efforts resulted in what is now seen as the great age of pyramid-building. One of these rulers built a step pyramid at Meidum, located several miles south of Sakkara. Later, another pharaoh filled in the notches of the Meidum pyramid's steps, creating the first smooth-sided pyramid. Seneferu, the first ruler of the Fourth Dynasty, built a number of pyramids. The most famous of these is the "Bent" Pyramid at Dahshur, situated between Sakkara and Meidum. The structure appears to be bent because the builders abruptly reduced the steepness of its sides when it was about half finished, making the top half of the pyramid smaller than was originally planned. The reason for this change is unknown. Some modern scholars think that Seneferu may have died during construction, prompting the next pharaoh to finish the tomb as quickly as possible.

This photograph shows the Bent Pyramid in Dahshur.

Generations of pharaohs created these marvels, which are considered to be some of the world's greatest monuments.

The largest, most impressive, and most famous pyramids of all were those of Seneferu's son, Khufu (whom the Greeks called Cheops), and grandson, Khafre (also called Chephren). These enormous structures still stand at Giza. The "Great Pyramid," which its builders called *Akhet-Khufu*, meaning "Khufu's Horizon," measures about 756 feet (230 m) on each of the four sides of its base. This base covers an area of more than 13 acres (5 hectares). The building's original height was 481 feet (147 m), more than two and a half times as high as New York's towering Statue of Liberty! Khafre's pyramid,

16

which looms nearby, is only slightly smaller than his father's. A third and considerably smaller pyramid at Giza is that of the pharaoh Menkaure, Khafre's successor.

Although many other pyramids rose in Egypt in the centuries that followed, none were nearly as large as those at Giza. Because these structures were extremely costly and time-consuming to build, pyramids grew increasingly smaller and fewer in number. By the end of the Middle Kingdom (about 1650 B.C.), Egyptian rulers had largely abandoned the building of pyramids.

These pyramids have stood as remarkable achievements of the ancient Egyptians for centuries. They are, from left to right, the pyramid of Menkaure, pyramid of Khafre, and the pyramid of Khufu (also known as the Great Pyramid). The smaller structures in the foreground are known as the queens' pyramids.

Chapter Two

The Pyramid Builders

The mighty pyramids at Giza are still more or less intact after thousands of years. But very little reliable information about the kings, designers, and workers who built these structures has survived. For a long time, most people assumed that what the ancient Greek historian Herodotus said about them was true. After he visited Egypt in the fifth century B.C., he wrote that Khufu and Khafre were cruel rulers. These pharaohs, the historian claimed, "brought the country into all sorts of misery" and forced their people "to labor as slaves" in building the great pyramids.

The problem with Herodotus's account is that he visited Egypt two thousand years after Khufu and Khafre died. The Greek writer faithfully reported what his Egyptian guides told him. But because so much time had passed since the pyramids had been built, the guides knew as little about their origins as Herodotus did. So much of what they told him was probably exaggerated or incorrect.

The Father of History

Herodotus was born in the Greek city of Halicarnassus in about 485 B.C. Today he is often called the "father of history," because he wrote the first known history book.

Preserving the Pharaoh's Body

Over the last two centuries, historians and other modern experts have provided some of the information that Herodotus lacked about the pyramid builders and their lives. First, cruel or not, Khufu and Khafre, like other Egyptian pharaohs, lived and died amid great wealth, luxury, and ceremony. In life, the king's word was law, and he commanded armies of both soldiers and government officials. They all considered him to be divine and knelt or bowed when approaching him.

In death, the pharaoh received the same high degree of respect he had in life. After Khufu died, his body was prepared for burial at the Valley Temple. This structure probably stood several hundred feet east of his pyramid. The temple was part of an elaborate complex of buildings, statues, and smaller tombs that originally surrounded the pharaoh's gigantic tomb.

The main task of those preparing the pharaoh's body for burial was to preserve it. Along with other Egyptians who could afford it, the pharaoh had his body preserved through the process of **mummification**. According to Herodotus, who learned how a mummy was created while he was in

This painting shows ancient Egyptians preparing a person for burial and building the sacrophagus to hold the body.

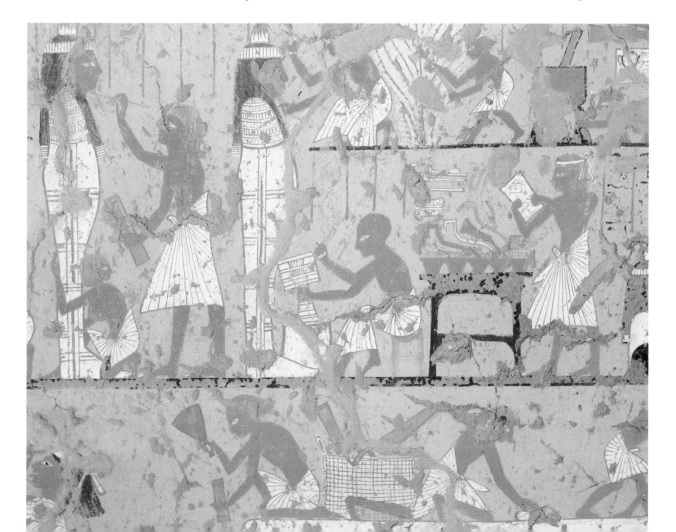

Egypt, "As much as possible of the brain is extracted through the nostrils with an iron hook." Next, he wrote, the front of the body "is laid open with a flint knife and the whole contents of the abdomen removed; the cavity is then thoroughly cleaned and washed out." Then the preparers placed the body in **natron**, a mineral salt that dried it out, and let it sit for seventy days. "When this period is over," Herodotus continued, "the body is washed and then wrapped from head to foot in linen cut into strips and smeared on the underside with gum."

A Royal Funeral

On the day of Khufu's funeral, a large group of priests, nobles, and servants gathered to honor his memory. In a stately **procession**, or orderly march, they solemnly carried the mummy to its final resting place inside the pyramid. The exact details of this ceremony are not known. But the mourners were probably dressed in their finest clothes. And it is likely that they sang a hymn similar to this one, which was found in the tomb of a later pharaoh:

> He is no longer upon the earth, he is in the sky! He rushes at the sky like a **heron**. He has kissed the sky like a **falcon**. He has leapt skyward like a grasshopper.

When Khufu's son, Khafre, died a generation later, his body was prepared in his own Valley Temple, located a few hundred yards south of Khufu's. By this time, the Giza complex included not only Khafre's new pyramid, but also the

The Great Sphinx

The Great Sphinx at Giza measures 240 feet (73 m) long and 66 feet (20 m) high. It has a lion's body and a human head. Many scholars think it was a portrait of King Khafre himself.

Great Sphinx. This huge statue was built atop a natural rock formation during Khafre's reign.

Architects and Workers

Great honor and respect were also given to the **architects** who designed and supervised the construction of the great stone tombs. Clearly, none of the pharaohs could have erected these gigantic monuments without the services of loyal and highly skilled architects. The first-known—and still most famous—of all Egyptian architects was Imhotep. He built the

Step Pyramid for King Djoser, launching the great pyramid age of the Old Kingdom.

Imhotep's reputation was great during his lifetime and even greater after his death. He received a magnificent funeral. And later generations of Egyptians worshiped him as a god, honoring him with his own temple in Memphis. Unfortunately, the names of the architects of the larger pyramids at Giza remain unknown.

As for the ordinary workers who followed the instructions of the royal architects, most were poor people who could not afford lavish burials. Usually, the body was wrapped in a **shroud** of linen or reeds and placed, along with some meager offerings of food, in a grave dug in the sand. Many such poor grave sites were **communal**, meaning that several persons were buried together. Over time, the arid desert conditions dried the bodies, sometimes preserving them for centuries.

These workers were not slaves, however, as Herodotus was told. Instead, they were free citizens, mostly farmers drafted for public work during the flood season when they could not

Imhotep designed the first pyramid and later became one of the Egyptian gods. He is said to have been the patron of scribes.

The Nile's Annual Floods

During the season of *akhet*, from June to September, the Nile River flooded. It covered the nearby farmlands with several feet of water and deposited a fresh layer of rich soil in the process. No one could farm during the flood season. So most people rested, worked at various crafts, or toiled on government-sponsored projects, including the construction of the pyramids.

work in their fields. During the reigns of Khufu and Khafre, the flood season witnessed a major migration of these laborers to Giza year after year. At least 10,000 and possibly as many as 20,000 of them worked on the pyramids of Giza. The laborers were organized into groups, or gangs, with colorful names such as the "Friends of Khufu" and the "Vigorous Gang." And each gang broke down into five smaller groups called **phyles**. A phyle had between ten and twenty men.

Ancient Egyptians worked in small groups to build the pyramids.

According to estimates, the Great Pyramid weighs close to 6 million tons.

Chapter Three

Building the Great Pyramid

The Great Pyramid of King Khufu remains one of the most massive structures in the world. About 2.3 million stone blocks, each weighing an average of 2.5 tons, went into its construction. This is more than five times the amount of stone used to make London's Westminster Abbey, one of the largest churches in the world. Another way of visualizing it is to imagine cutting up Khufu's tomb into 1-foot (30.5-cm) stone cubes. If you placed all these cubes in a row, they would stretch two-thirds of the way around the Earth!

What makes the building of this huge structure so amazing is that the ancient Egyptians accomplished it with very primitive **technology**—they did not have the modern tools and methods used to make things. They had no pulleys, for example, and did not use the wheel. And they also had no iron for making strong tools. (Iron tools and weapons did not come into wide use until about 1,400 years later.) Their chisels and saws were made of copper. Because this metal is much softer than iron, it bends and breaks more easily. Moreover, the hammers the Egyptians used were made of stone or wood rather than metal.

However, the Egyptians had two important advantages that made up for their lack of technology. These were abundant manpower and plenty of patience. Employing huge numbers of workers for periods of many years, they were

Methods for Obtaining Metals

The Egyptians mined copper **ore**—the rocks containing deposits of copper—in Nubia, the region south of Egypt, and in the Sinai Peninsula at the northern edge of the Red Sea. They heated the ore to a temperature of 700 degrees Fahrenheit (371 degrees Celsius) or more to melt the copper and separate the metal from the rocks. They also made **bronze**, an **alloy**, or mixture, of copper and another metal, tin. Adding a little tin to copper made it a harder and more durable material. Mining the ores and making metal tools, weapons, and other objects was very expensive, so the kings and nobles controlled most of the industry.

able to erect immense structures that today would require the use of advanced machinery.

Neya

Measuring the Site

As a first step in building a stone pyramid, workers used long cords to mark out a square on the surface of the construction site. The sides of the square formed a giant outline of the pyramid's base. In the case of Khufu's tomb, this step was carried out with incredible **precision**, or accuracy. Modern calculations show that the pyramid's base is less than 8 inches (20 centimeters) short of being a perfect square.

The next step was to make sure that the ground beneath the base was perfectly level so that the immense weight of the structure would be distributed evenly. Otherwise, there would be a danger of the pyramid collapsing. To level the site, the builders utilized the well-known fact that the surface of standing water is always perfectly level. First, workers dug trenches around the site. Next, they filled the trenches with water. Using the water's level as a standard, they determined where the ground needed to be higher or lower. Their leveling calculations from one side of the pyramid to the other were off by a mere 0.5 inch (1.2 cm)!

Facing North

For reasons that are still unclear to us, the architects made sure that the entrance of the Great Pyramid at Giza would face the North Star. That star always remains above the horizon in Egypt.

Cutting and Moving the Stones

While the ground was being marked and leveled, other workers cut and hauled the stone blocks for the pyramid's lower courses, or levels. Most of the stone for the Great Pyramid

Many of the stones needed for Khufu's pyramid were brought to the site by boat.

came from quarries located a few hundred yards south of the structure. However, some of the blocks came from as far away as Aswan, nearly 500 miles (800 km) to the south. These blocks had to be floated on barges down the Nile River to the Giza work site.

At the quarries, cutting the giant stones was an extremely difficult task. Copper tools were not strong enough, so workers drove wooden wedges into cracks in the quarry walls and soaked the wood with water. The water made the wedges expand, which widened the cracks and split off large chunks of stone. Another method was to heat the cracks and then splash them with cold water. The sudden change in temperature often caused the cracks to expand, loosening chunks of rock. Using hammers and chisels, the other workers then spent many long hours and days chipping the chunks into the desired rectangular shape.

Moving the enormous stones also required a great deal of time, effort, and patience. First, workers drove a thick wooden pole under one side of a stone block and used the pole as a

This painting shows ancient Egyptians dragging stone blocks for a building project.

The Structures Surrounding Khufu's Pyramid

A long, straight stone **causeway**, or ramp, led from the Valley Temple on the edge of the river to the Great Pyramid. A temple for worshiping the pharaoh's spirit stood near the structure's base. Small pyramids and mastabas to hold the bodies of other members of the royal family stood nearby.

lever to lift that side of the block up a few inches. Other workers quickly slipped logs underneath the block. Using strong ropes made of reeds, the men then dragged the block across the logs, which acted like rollers. As the block moved slowly forward, two men kept rotating the logs from back to front. Meanwhile, another man poured a liquid, probably oil or milk, over the logs and stones to make them slide more easily over one another. Then, using these methods, it probably took about ten to twelve workers to move one of these massive blocks along level ground.

The Structure Grows Steadily Higher

Moving the stone blocks upward was more difficult than transporting them over level ground. As the pyramid grew increasingly higher, much larger groups of workers were needed to drag the blocks up to the top course. They accomplished this tremendous feat by building huge earthen ramps around the sides of the structure. Teams of men, sometimes aided by oxen, pulled the blocks up the ramps to the top course and fitted them into place. When that course was completed, they increased the height of the ramps and started laying the next layer.

As the structure rose steadily higher, other groups of workers dragged large pieces of pure white limestone up the ramps. They wedged these "casing stones" into place over the outer edges of the courses. Then they carefully polished them, giving the pyramid a smooth, gleaming, and beautiful outside surface. The casing stones fitted together so precisely that it was difficult to drive a knife-blade between them. When workers installed the topmost block, a triangular, pointed piece called the **capstone**, the pyramid was finished. Thousands of workers then labored for weeks—or perhaps months—to remove the massive earthen ramps, finally revealing to the world the great monument in its original and magnificent glory.

Ramps were used to get the stones to the different levels of the pyramid.

Visitors explore the inside of the Great Pyramid, navigating the passageway from the second to third gallery.

Chapter Four

Inside the Great Pyramid

While the outside of the Great Pyramid of Khufu was a marvel to behold, the design and construction of the inside, where the pharaoh's body was meant to rest for eternity, was no less impressive. In most Egyptian pyramids, the inner architecture was fairly simple. In Khafre's tomb, for example, a few passages lead to a single burial chamber underneath the structure. By contrast, the Great Pyramid contains many corridors and chambers.

Just an Illusion

Khafre's pyramid was built on higher ground than Khufu's, so it often produces the illusion that it is taller than the Great Pyramid.

Chambers and Galleries

Originally, like Djoser, Khafre, and others, Khufu planned for a simple burial chamber beneath the pyramid. When this chamber was only partly completed, however, he evidently changed his mind and work began on a room farther up, within the structure itself. This became known as the "Queen's Chamber," even though it was never intended for Khufu's wife. The roof of this room was finished and its floor was about to be laid when the pharaoh changed his mind again. Several feet above the Queen's Chamber, workers added the "Grand Gallery," a room sloping upward at an angle toward the center of the pyramid.

The Grand Gallery is a highly impressive piece of engineering. It is 153 feet (46 m) long, 28 feet (8.5 m) high, and has a corbeled roof. In **corbeling**, layers of stone are stacked so that each layer slightly overhangs the one below it. When the layers finally meet at the top, they form a corbeled arch or vault.

The Grand Gallery leads to the so-called "King's Chamber," which was Khufu's final resting place. The architects wanted to make sure that the immense weight of the pyramid's

Mysterious Passageways

Two narrow **shafts**, or passageways, lead out of the King's Chamber in Khufu's pyramid. Two more shafts lead out of the Queen's Chamber. These shafts are too small for a person to crawl through. The exact purpose of these passageways remains a mystery.

Men work by torchlight inside the king's chamber, which is lined in granite.

upper levels would not cause the chamber's roof to collapse and crush the pharaoh's mummy. For this reason, they constructed five compartments, one atop another, directly above the King's Chamber. Because these compartments are hollow, they greatly reduce the weight pressing down on the chamber's roof. They have certainly done their job, for after some forty-six centuries the King's Chamber remains intact.

The Problem of Tomb Robbers

Unfortunately, although the King's Chamber has survived the ages, its original contents have not. Only a few hundred years after Khufu's funeral, tomb robbers broke into the pyramid. Such robbers were an ever present fact of life in ancient Egypt, and over the centuries they looted almost every royal tomb in the country. The thieves who entered Khufu's pyramid either stole or destroyed the pharaoh's mummy. They also took all of

Tomb robbers steal gold and other items from the tomb of a pharaoh.

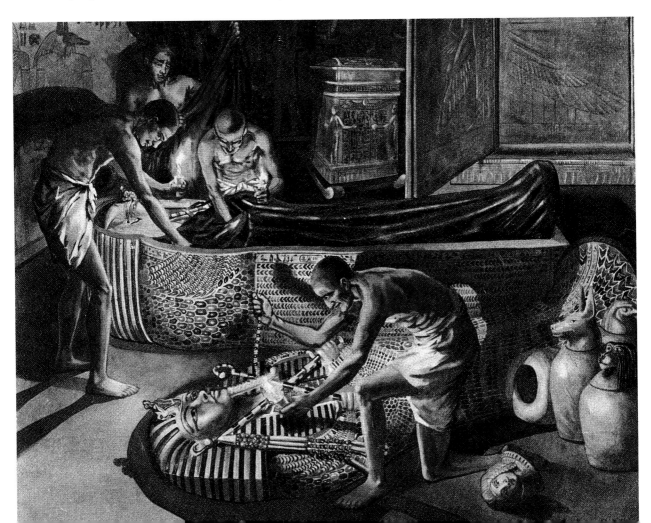

The Dead King Dwells with the Gods

After the death of Tuthmosis II, a pharaoh of the eighteenth dynasty, one of his court officials wrote: "Having ascended into heaven, he became united with the gods, and his son, having arisen in his place as king of the Two Lands [Upper and Lower Egypt], ruled on the throne of his father."

the thousands of artifacts that probably once crowded the burial vault.

The custom of filling a king's tomb with thousands of material objects grew out of deeply held religious beliefs. The Egyptians thought that after a pharaoh died he dwelled eternally with the other gods. And because of his divinity, it was thought that he should be able to enjoy the same material splendor in death as he did in life. Therefore, the burial offerings in royal tombs included more than just food, drink, and clothes. They also contained fine jewelry, elaborately decorated thrones and other furniture, vases, weapons, chariots, full-sized boats, and other items.

A Pharaoh's Treasures Found Intact

A fabulous discovery made in Egypt in modern times fortunately gives us some idea of how Khufu's burial chamber probably looked at the moment the workers sealed it. In 1922, Howard Carter, a British **archaeologist** (a person who studies ancient civilizations), was working in the Valley of the Kings—a remote rocky area on the Nile's west bank several hundred miles south of Giza. Attempting to keep their remains safe

Dr. Howard Carter examines King Tutankhamun's sarcophagus. He spent nearly ten years recovering and recording all of the items he found in the tomb.

from robbers, many pharaohs created secret tombs in the valley's cliffs. Over time, however, thieves successfully found and plundered even these hidden royal burial chambers.

Carter unearthed the only royal tomb in the Valley of the Kings that escaped complete pillage. It was the final resting place of the pharaoh Tutankhamun, popularly known as "King Tut," who reigned from 1336 to 1327 B.C. On entering the tomb, which consists of several chambers, Carter saw that robbers had broken in shortly after the funeral. But for reasons unknown, they had stolen only a few small objects. Perhaps guards chased them away before they could take more. Almost all of the pharaoh's treasure—more than 2,000 artifacts in all—still remained in their original positions.

In addition to weapons, furniture, jewelry, musical instruments, boats, and much more, Carter found Tut's mummy. It lay inside a solid-gold coffin. This magnificent container rested inside a second coffin, which was made of wood covered by a layer of gold. And this second coffin was itself encased by a third. Considering that Khufu and Khafre were much more powerful and important kings than Tut, we can safely assume that their burial vaults were even richer and more beautiful than his.

This photograph shows the innermost coffin in King Tutankamun's tomb.

Carter's First Glimpse of Tut's Treasures

Howard Carter later recalled the exciting moment when he inserted a candle into a small hole and first saw the interior of King Tut's tomb: "[My colleague] asked, 'Can you see anything?' It was all I could do to get out the words, 'Yes, wonderful things!'"

While the mummy of Ahmose was discovered in Deir el-Bahri in 1881, no one has found his tomb.

Chapter Five

The Survival of the Pyramids

As time went on, the ancient Egyptians made fewer and fewer pyramids, all of them much smaller than the ones at Giza. The last pyramid built in Egypt was possibly that of the pharaoh Ahmose, who reigned from 1550 to 1525 B.C. The structure was part of a funerary temple he erected near Thebes, a city located on the Nile about 330 miles (530 km) south of Giza. A stone **causeway** almost 0.75 mile (1.2 km) long led to the temple, which was square-shaped and had three levels. Each of the first two levels featured a **colonnade**—a row of columns—running along its outer perimeter. Forming the third level, in the center, was the pyramid. It was perhaps 30 to 40 feet (9 to 12 m) tall and solid, having no interior chambers or corridors. The location of Ahmose's tomb is uncertain, but it may have been situated a few hundred feet away beneath a cliff.

Egypt Gets a New City

In the 330s B.C., the Greek conqueror Alexander the Great liberated Egypt from the Persians, who had held the country for more than two centuries. He established the city of Alexandria, named after himself, near the mouth of the Nile. For several centuries afterward, under Greek and Roman rule, Alexandria was one of the economic and cultural centers of the known world.

Ahmose's relatively small pyramid was already nearly three hundred years old when King Tut was laid to rest in the Valley of the Kings. As the centuries rolled on, Egyptian civilization steadily declined in power and influence. A succession of foreign peoples seized control of the country, including Ethiopians, Assyrians, Persians, Greeks, Romans, and Muslims. These peoples had little or no interest in Egypt's past glories and did not bother to maintain many of the older palaces and other structures. More often they constructed new palaces or even entire new cities for themselves.

The Pyramids Shrouded in Mystery

During the long centuries of foreign rule in Egypt, robbers continued to loot what few treasures were left in the pyramids. And because no one guarded or repaired these monuments any more, they slowly eroded and decayed, some of them crumbling into mere mounds of rubble. At the same time, various rulers ordered the fine limestone casing stones stripped from the pyramids. They used these stones to build new houses and palaces.

By early modern times, no one remembered exactly who had built the surviving pyramids or even knew the original purpose of these structures. Also, Egypt had become a very poor country. Many European visitors viewed the modern Egyptians as primitive and found it difficult to imagine that their ancestors could have built the impressive Giza pyramids on their own.

Founder of the New Kingdom

The pharaoh Ahmose is famous for helping to drive the Hyksos, a group of foreign invaders, out of Egypt. He then established the eighteenth dynasty, which began the period that modern scholars call the New Kingdom (1550–1070 B.C.).

As the centuries passed, the pyramids became forgotten relics of an ancient time.

For these reasons, an air of mystery grew up around the origins, purposes, builders, and construction of the pyramids. To answer the many questions asked about these structures, people proposed some unusual and even bizarre theories. Some suggested that the pyramids were vaults where mysterious ancient **sages**, or wise men, stored their writings. Others claimed the pyramids were grain storehouses erected by the biblical character Joseph or giant models of Noah's Ark. Some thought the pyramids were observatories for studying the stars and planets, or computer-like devices containing a secret code that could predict important historical events.

Modern Scholars Reveal Egypt's Past

Eventually, archaeologists, historians, and scientists proved that a powerful and brilliant civilization had once existed in Egypt. They confirmed that some of the ancient pharaohs were great builders. Evidence showed that these rulers had marshaled the efforts of thousands of their subjects to erect huge palaces and temples as well as pyramids, which they used as tombs. The first detailed modern scientific investigation of the Great Pyramid was carried out in the late 1800s by Britain's Sir William Flinders Petrie. By examining evidence found inside and outside the pyramids, he and later scholars offered logical explanations for how the early Egyptians had created these structures.

Sir William Flinders Petrie spent two years studying the pyramids of Giza.

Yet even today, some people refuse to accept the evidence. Insisting that there is something mysterious about the pyramids, they continue to put forward wild notions about them. One such idea suggests that the knowledge needed to build the Great Pyramid came from an extremely ancient society possessing technology more advanced than today's. In his book *Worlds Before Our Own*, writer Brad Steiger asks, "Were the pyramids built by architects from [the lost continent of] Atlantis? Is the Great Pyramid. . . the physical embodiment [material example] of a lost science?" Some people go so far as to claim that alien beings from other planets either built the pyramids or showed the Egyptians how to build them. So far, those making such claims have failed to provide any

Pioneer of Egyptian Archaeology

Sir William Flinders Petrie (1853–1942) was the first modern archaeologist to work in Egypt. He uncovered the tombs of the kings of the first and second dynasties and thoroughly explored and measured the pyramids at Giza.

Much of the evidence points to the Egyptians as the builders of the pyramids.

convincing evidence. Meanwhile, new evidence confirming that the Egyptians built the pyramids themselves using primitive methods continues to be found.

Eternal Symbols of Past Greatness

While people continue to argue about how the pyramids came to be, everyone agrees on one point—the sight of these ancient structures stirs the heart and the imagination. Each year, thousands of people travel from all over the world to

A New Discovery

In March 1999, Dr. Zahi Hawass, one of Egypt's leading archaeologists announced the discovery of an ancient coffin at Giza, about 1/2 mile (0.8 km) from the Great Pyramid of Khufu. Evidence found both on and in the coffin shows that the mummy inside is the remains of Kai, a high priest of the royal court.

Egypt to see, touch, and even climb them. In fact, the Giza pyramids, along with the Great Sphinx, are the most popular sites with visitors to Egypt.

However, other smaller pyramids are also popular sites. In 1996, the Egyptian government opened the eleven pyramids at Dahshur, including the Bent Pyramid, to the public. It is tempting to wonder what the pharaohs, architects, and workers who built the pyramids would think of the crowds of

Each year, the amazing sight of the pyramids draws thousands of visitors.

people from many lands flocking to view the huge tombs. Perhaps they would be proud to learn that after so many centuries the fruits of their labor still tower over the Nile, majestic and eternal symbols of their society's greatness.

Timeline

B.C.	
ca. 3150–3100	A powerful ruler named Menes unites the kingdoms of Upper and Lower Egypt, creating the world's first true nation.
2700–2180	These are the years of the Old Kingdom, during which most of Egypt's pyramids are built, including the largest ones, at Giza (near modern Cairo).
2598–2566	Reign of the pharaoh Khufu who erects the largest of all the pyramids for his tomb.
2050–1650	These are the years of the Middle Kingdom, in which the Egyptians begin expanding their territory by conquest.
1550–1070	These are the years of the New Kingdom, in which a series of vigorous pharaohs create an Egyptian empire.
1550–1525	The Pharaoh Ahmose reigns, whose small pyramid was probably the last one built by an Egyptian ruler.
1336–1327	The pharaoh Tutankhamun reigns, popularly known today as "King Tut."
323	The Greek conqueror Alexander the Great dies. His armies had entered Egypt a few years earlier. Following his death, one of his generals, Ptolemy, makes himself pharaoh of Egypt, beginning a Greek royal line.
31	Cleopatra VII, last of the Ptolemies, and the last independent ruler of Egypt, is defeated by the Romans at Actium, in Greece. The following year, she commits suicide and Rome makes Egypt a province in its own empire.

continued next page

Timeline *continued*

A.D.	
1798	The French conqueror Napoleon invades Egypt. He brings along more than a hundred scholars to study the country's ancient monuments.
1799	The Rosetta Stone is discovered, which proves to be the key to deciphering hieroglyphics, the picture language used by the ancient Egyptians.
1853–1942	The life of William Flinders Petrie, the first modern archaeologist to explore Egypt's ancient monuments. He thoroughly measures and studies the pyramids at Giza.
1922	English archaeologist Howard Carter unearths King Tut's tomb, filled with golden artifacts, a find that creates a worldwide sensation.
1999	A coffin containing the remains of an Egyptian high priest named Kai is discovered near the great pyramid of Khufu.

Glossary

akhet—the season lasting from June through September, when the Nile River flooded in Egypt

alloy—a mixture of metals

archaeologist—a person who studies ancient civilizations and their artifacts

architect—a person who designs buildings and other structures

arid—dry

ba—the part of a person's soul representing the personality in ancient Egypt

bronze—a metal alloy made by mixing copper and tin

capstone—the triangular, pointed block that forms the top of a pyramid

causeway—a ramp or walkway

colonnade—a row of columns

communal—shared by members of a group

corbeling—a method of making roofs in which layers of stone are stacked so that each layer slightly overhangs the one below

dynasty—a line of rulers belonging to the same family

falcon—a large hunting bird considered sacred in Egypt. It is also called a hawk.

heron—a large wading bird with a long bill and soft feathers

immortality—eternal life

ka—the part of a person's soul believed to represent the life force in ancient Egypt

mastaba—a low, rectangular tomb made of mud bricks or stone

mausoleum—a large stone tomb

mummification—a process used by the ancient Egyptians and other peoples to preserve dead bodies

natron—a mineral salt used in ancient times to dry out bodies

ore—a rock that contains metal, such as copper or tin

papyrus—paper made from sedge, a water plant that grows in the Nile Valley

pharaoh—a king of ancient Egypt. The word came from the term *per-aa*, meaning "great house," which was probably a reference to the large, luxurious palaces these rulers built for themselves.

phyle—a group of ten to twenty Egyptian workers. Five phyles formed a gang.

precision—accuracy

procession—a ceremonial march or a parade

sage—a wise person

shaft—a narrow passageway or tunnel inside a building or underground

shroud—a cloth used to wrap up a dead body for burial

technology—the tools and methods used to make things

trademark—a major identifying feature of a person, place, or thing

To Find Out More

Books

Casson, Lionel. *Daily Life in Ancient Egypt.* New York: American Heritage, 1975.

———. *Ancient Egypt.* New York: Time-Life Books, 1965.

Clare, John, D., ed. *Pyramids of Ancient Egypt.* New York: Harcourt Brace Jovanovich, 1992.

Donnelly, Judy. *Tut's Mummy, Lost. . . And Found.* New York: Random House, 1988.

Martell, Hazel M. *The Ancient World: From the Ice Age to the Fall of Rome.* New York: Kingfisher, 1995.

Millard, Anne. *Mysteries of the Pyramids.* Brookfield, CT: Millbrook Press, 1995.

Mitchell, Barbara. *Pyramids: Opposing Viewpoints.* St. Paul: Greenhaven Press, 1988.

Nardo, Don. *Cleopatra.* San Diego: Lucent Books, 1994.

Reeves, Nicholas. *Into the Mummy's Tomb.* New York: Scholastic/Madison Press, 1992.

Woods, Geraldine. *Science in Ancient Egypt.* New York: Franklin Watts, 1988.

Organizations and Online Sources

The Metropolitan Museum of Art
1000 Fifth Avenue
New York, NY 10028
http://www.metmuseum.org
Explore ancient Egypt through this museum's collection. Its online site includes many artifacts, and even has a section called "Egyptian Art in the Age of the Pyramids."

Museum of Fine Arts
Avenue of the Arts
465 Huntington Avenue
Boston, MA 02115-5523
http://www.mfa.org
The museum's online site has a special section called "Pharaohs of the Sun" where visitors can learn more about ancient Egypt.

The Pyramids

http://www.touregypt.net/construction

Provides information about the design and construction of Egypt's famous pyramids.

The Pyramids—The Inside Story

http://www.pbs.org/wgbh/nova/pyramid

This excellent site, sponsored by the first-rate TV science program NOVA, contains a great deal of up-to-date information about the pyramids, including interviews with experts.

Tour Egypt

http://www.memphis.edu/egypt/egypt.html

This educational tour of Egyptian places includes links for Giza, the site of the Great Pyramid, and Egypt's modern capital of Cairo.

University of Pennsylvania Museum of Archaeology and Anthropology
Thirty-third and Spruce Streets
Philadelphia, PA 19104

http://www.upenn.edu/museum/index.html

This museum's online site provides information on ancient Egyptian culture, and includes fun activities, such as how to write your name in hieroglyphics.

A Note on Sources

The Egyptian pyramids are among the most famous and awe-inspiring works humanity has ever produced. So it should come as no surprise that a tremendous amount of material has been written about them over the years. One of the most valuable modern studies of these monuments is *The Pyramids of Egypt*, written in the 1940s by I. E. S. Edwards, one of the twentieth century's leading experts on ancient Egypt. The work is now somewhat dated because new information and theories about the pyramids have appeared since that time. However, it remains essential reading on the subject; and I consulted it in preparing this book. I have also looked at more recent books about the pyramids, along with some articles in scholarly journals.

It would be a mistake, however, to consider the pyramids outside of the larger context of Egyptian history and culture. This is because they were a special product of that unique culture, its religious beliefs, and the singular physical setting of ancient Egypt. One of the best recent general overviews of ancient Egyptian history is Nicolas Grimal's *History of Ancient Egypt*, which I consulted often. And for cultural aspects, H. W. F. Saggs' *Civilization Before Greece and Rome* is excellent. Several worthwhile books about everyday life in ancient Egypt have been published in the last thirty years. Two of the better ones are by scholars Lionel Casson and Barbara Mertz, both of which I used in writing this volume.

—*Don Nardo*

Index

Numbers in *italics* indicate illustrations.

About the Author

Don Nardo is a historian and award-winning writer who has published numerous books about the ancient world. Among these are *The Age of Pericles*, about the golden age of ancient Greece; *The Battle of Marathon*, which tells the exciting story of how the soldiers of ancient Athens defeated a much larger force of invading Persians; *Life of a Roman Soldier*, a fascinating study of the ancient Roman military; *Empires of Mesopotamia*, an overview of the ancient Sumerians, Babylonians, and Assyrians; and biographies of the great Roman general, Julius Caesar, and the wily Egyptian queen, Cleopatra. Mr. Nardo lives with his wife Christine in Massachusetts.